BECAUSEYOUCARE

Celebrating Nurses, Caregivers and Other Everyday Heroes.

Compiled by Dan Zadra
Designed by Steve Potter and Jenica Wilkie

COMPENDIUM
PUBLISHING

live inspired.

ACKNOWLEDGEMENTS

These quotations were gathered lovingly but unscientifically over several years and or contributed by many friends or acquaintances. Some arrived—and survived in our files—on scraps of paper and may therefore be imperfectly worded or attributed. To the authors, contributors and original sources, our thanks, and where appropriate, our apologies. —The Editors

WITH SPECIAL THANKS TO

Jason Aldrich, Gerry Baird, Jay Baird, Neil Beaton, Josie Bissett, Jan Catey, Doug Cruickshank, Jim Darragh, Jennifer & Matt Ellison, Rob Estes, Michael Flynn & Family, Shannan Frisbie, Jennifer Hurwitz, Heidi Jones, Cristal & Brad Olberg, Janet Potter & Family, Diane Roger, Jenica Wilkie, Clarie Yam & Erik Lee, Kobi, Heidi & Shale Yamada, Justi, Tote & Caden Yamada, Robert & Val Yamada, Kaz, Kristin, Kyle & Kendyl Yamada, Tai & Joy Yamada, Anne Zadra, August & Arline Zadra.

CREDITS

Compiled by Dan Zadra
Designed by Steve Potter & Jenica Wilkie

In the deserts of the
heart let the healing
fountain start.

—W.H. Auden

Heroes in Our Midst

No one goes through life without being touched by the angels—
our nurses and caregivers. We all have stories.

I remember when my son was born. Our nurse worked side-by-side
with us all night long; it was so beautiful and so exhausting for everyone.
Somehow she made us feel as if she cared as much as we did—that ours
was the first and only baby she had ever delivered, the only one in the
world who really mattered that night.

I remember when my daughter had ear surgery. She was just five years
old and looked too tiny to have an operation. The nurse knew how
nervous I was, so she let me push my daughter's gurney to the O.R.
Somehow she made me feel as if my daughter was her daughter too,
and that nothing bad could possibly happen.

BECAUSE

I remember when my father was in his eighties. He fell in the rain outside his church and couldn't get up. He was sad, scared and embarrassed—but then the ambulance came. Somehow those big strong guys were so tender. They understood Dad's feelings, got him back on his feet, and then led the onlookers in a round of applause!

I remember when Dad was 96 and had come home from the hospital to spend his last Christmas with us. We all knew that he only had a few days to live. But somehow his Hospice nurses and caregivers made those final days feel so full and rich. Because of them, some of our Christmas gifts that year were strength, courage, wisdom, faith, forgiveness, healing, peace, joy, laughter and love.

I am so grateful to these wonderful, caring people. We all are.

Dan Zadra

YOUCARE

I'm proud and honored to be a patient here. Your nurses deserve a trophy with a gold heart on it. My daughter says she wants to be just like you, nothing would make me prouder.

PURPOSE

The purpose of life is a life of purpose.

—Robert Byrne

All of us are born for a reason, but all of us
don't discover why. Success in life has nothing
to do with what you gain or accomplish for
yourself. It's what you do for others.

—Danny Thomas,
for St. Jude Hospital

I don't know what your destiny will be,
but this I know: the only ones among you
who will be truly happy are those who will
have sought and found how to serve.

—Albert Schweitzer

I don't think there's anything as
wonderful in life, or as challenging,
as being called to help others.

—Betty Ford

Nursing is the hardest and
easiest thing I've ever done.

—Sally Karioth, RN

The first two rules of becoming a caregiver:
1) It will be difficult. 2) It will be worth it.

—O.C. School of Medicine

BECAUSE

You will be mentally stressed. You will be emotionally challenged. You will learn how to work together. You will learn to work alone. You will learn when to speak. You will learn when to be silent. You will learn when to lead. You will learn when to follow. You will be constructively criticized. You will be praised. You will shed a few tears. You will share in each other's laughter. You will learn the need to help each other. You will learn to help yourself. You will learn to be part of a group. You will learn to be yourself—an individual. You will learn responsibility. You will learn discipline. You will learn these things because someday someone's life will depend on you. You are a nursing student. You will graduate. You will be, in all its wonder and glory, a Nurse.

—Anneliese Garrison, RN,
"You Are A Nursing Student"

YOUCARE

The best way to find
yourself is to lose yourself
in the service of others.

— Mohandas K. Gandhi

Finding the right work
is like discovering your
soul in the world.

— Thomas Moore

Nothing liberates our greatness like
the desire to help, the desire to serve.

— Marianne Williamson

BECAUSE

Without you, someone may not be living.

—Sandy Medica, RN

Knowing that we can make a difference
in this world is a great motivator.
How can we know this and not be involved?

—Susan Jeffers

One who saves one life
is counted as if they have
saved the entire world.

—The Torah

YOUCARE

WHEN I CAME TO THE HOSPITAL
I WAS DOWNHEARTED AND
AFRAID BUT YOU GAVE ME BACK
MY COURAGE. I FEEL LIKE
THE LION FROM WIZARD OF
OZ. I'M GOING HOME NOW—
I CAN'T THANK YOU ENOUGH.

COURAGE

How very little can be done
under the spirit of fear.

—Florence Nightingale

It takes courage for people to listen
to their own goodness and act on it.

—Pablo Casals

Life becomes harder for us
when we live for others, but it also
becomes richer and happier.

—Albert Schweitzer

Feeling requires courage.

—Helen Keller

Caring takes guts.
Every morning I remind myself,
"I meet my work with strong arms,
open hands, courageous heart."

—Connie Price, RN, Emergency

Courage is not the absence of
fear and pain, but the affirmation
of life despite fear and pain.

—Rabbi Earl Grollman

BECAUSE

Grace under pressure.

—Ernest Hemingway

The bravest are the tenderest,
the loving are the daring.

—Bayard Taylor

Our caregivers carry this quote by Mother Teresa.
It was meant to be shared with our patients,
but it's a great affirmation for staff, too:
"I know God won't give me anything I can't handle,
I just wish He didn't trust me so much."

—Terri Atkinson, Hospice

YOUCARE

I may be compelled to face danger,
but never fear it, and while our soldiers
can stand and fight, I can stand
and feed and nurse them.

—Clara Barton, Civil War Nurse and
founder of the Red Cross

There is only one place for the women who
served and that is on the same site with our brother
soldiers. These women have touched thousands
of those names on the (Vietnam) wall. We have to be
at that spot, physically, spiritually and emotionally.

—Diane Carlson Evans, U.S. Nurse

BECAUSE

Everyday courage has few witnesses.
But yours is no less noble because no
drum beats before you, and no
crowds shout your name.

—Robert Louis Stevenson

If the world is to be healed through
human efforts, I am convinced it will be by
ordinary people—people whose love for this
life is even greater than their fears.

—Joanna Macy

YOUCARE

I woke up to a living nightmare of a stroke. I couldn't talk or even ask for what I needed. Would anyone care? Your fantastic nurses cared every day. They touched me, I'll never forget.

COMPASSION

The greatest tragedy is indifference.

— The Red Cross

The biggest disease today is not
leprosy or tuberculosis, but rather
the feeling of being unwanted.

— Mother Teresa

What matters in today's world is not
the difference between those who believe and
those who do not believe, but the difference
between those who care and those who don't.

— Abbe Pire

We run this hospital with our
hearts, it's not our culture to be
complacent in caring for a patient.

—Peggy Birdseye, RN

We are here to add to the
sum of human goodness.
To prove the thing exists.

—Josephine Hart

The work of our heart, the work of
taking time to listen, to help, is also
our gift to the whole of the world.

—Jack Kornfield

BECAUSE

The first duty of
compassion is to listen.

—Elizabeth David

Empathy is your pain
I feel in my heart.

—Hospice Volunteer

The greatest object in the universe, says the
philosopher, is a good person struggling
with adversity; yet there is a greater, which is
the good person who comes to relieve it.

—Oliver Goldsmith

YOUCARE

Without a sense of caring, there
can be no sense of community.

—Anthony J. D'Angelo

Too many people do not care
what happens as long as it
does not happen to them.

—William Howard Taft

The moral test of a society is how that
society treats those who are in the dawn of life—
the children; those who are in the twilight of life—
the elderly; and those who are in the shadow of life—the sick,
the needy, the handicapped.

—Hubert Humphrey

BECAUSE

We can't help everyone, but
everyone can help someone.

—Dr. Loretta Scott

When you go out into this world remember:
compassion, compassion, compassion.

—Betty Williams, Nobel Peace Laureate

It is only in watching nurses weave the tapestry
of care that we grasp its integrity and its meaning
for a society that too easily forgets the value
of things that are beyond price.

—Suzanne Gordon,
"What Nurses Stand For"

I'm hopeless with names, but I remember all of you. Believe me I remember your smiles and your tenderness. I'm sure you have better things to do than take care of me, but you'd never know it.

COMFORT

Care is a verb.

—Clara Billings

What value has
compassion if it does not
take its object in its arms?

—Antoine de Saint-Exupery

Sympathy sees and says, "I'm sorry."
Compassion sees and says, "I'll help."

—Elizabeth David

We need heart-to-heart resuscitation.

—Ram Dass

Inscribed on the lamp outside
Albert Schweitzer's jungle hospital:
"Here, at whatever hour you come,
you will find light and help
and human kindness."

—Caregivers West

Encouragement is the oxygen of the soul.

—Unknown

BECAUSE

Words of comfort,
skillfully administered, are the
oldest medicine known to man.

—Louis Nizer

Posted by the nursing staff at St. Anthony's Health
Center: "Yes I'm a patient, but don't avoid me just
because I'm ill. Be the friend, the loved one, you've
always been. Weep with me when I weep. Laugh with
me when I laugh. Don't be afraid to share this with me.
Call me first but don't be afraid to visit. I need you, I get
lonely. Bring me a positive attitude—it's catching!
Help me celebrate today, tomorrow—life!"

—LeAnn Malone

YOUCARE

If I don't get emotionally involved
with my patients, it's time for
me to change professions.

—Sally Karioth, RN

There are spaces between our fingers so that
another person's fingers can fill them in.

—Unknown

Loving touch makes the difference. Without Mom's chicken
soup, without Mother Teresa, without the
loving touch of our neighbor in church or a caress
in the hospital, we are ultimately lost.

—Everett Tetley

BECAUSE

Go ahead and cry.
I'll catch your tears.

—Jilleen Russell

If someone listens, or stretches out
a hand, or whispers a kind word of
encouragement, or attempts to understand,
extraordinary things begin to happen.

—Loretta Girzartis

Although the world is full of suffering,
it is also full of the overcoming of it.

—Helen Keller

YOUCARE

You taught us that sometimes you have to make your own sunshine. My husband says it best: In two months at the hospital we often felt helpless but we never felt hopeless. Thank you, one and all.

HOPE

Always leave the door open for hope.

Thank God I had doctors and nurses
who fueled and protected my hope. I call
hope my pilot light, for I now know that
without it I truly cease to exist.

Hope is a good thing,
maybe the best of things, and
no good thing ever dies.

Through the centuries we faced
down death by daring to hope.

—Maya Angelou

The bravest sight in all this world is
someone fighting against the odds.

—Franklin Lane

A hospital chaplain once told me, "There are no
hopeless situations; there are only people who
have grown hopeless about them."

—Dan Baker, Kitsap EMT

BECAUSE

It is at night that faith in
light is most admirable.
—Edmond Rostand

We have come to realize that our patients
can live with the word 'incurable', but they cannot
live without the word, HOPE! What every patient
needs from friends, family, nurses and physicians is
a ringing endorsement of HOPE—and a constant
reminder of the truth. The truth is, no matter what
the odds say about a particular illness, those
odds are being beaten all the time.
—Nurses' Helpline

YOUCARE

Laughter is an
essential amino acid.

—Patch Adams, MD

I have a dream—a vision of how
caring could be. That tears could
give way to laughter...that joy could
surface in our sadness.

—Ronna Fay Jevne

I would look up and
laugh, and love, and lift.

—Howard A. Wheeler

BECAUSE

Hope is the voice of the heart.

—Copernicus

Laughter in the face of reality is probably
the finest sound there is. In fact, a good
time to laugh is any time you can.

—Linda Ellerbee
(while fighting cancer)

Lend me your hope for awhile.
A time will come when I will heal, and I
will lend my renewed hope to others.

—Eloise Cole

YOUCARE

Because of you I am a survivor. I really believe that your nurses and aids loved me through it. It was so hard for me to accept the love and care at first — but when I finally did I got well.

LOVE

Some people care so much.
I think it's called love.

—Pooh

A job is what we do for money;
our work is what we do for love.

—Marysarah Quinn

Angel Rest Stop: Halos polished
and straightened … Wings fluffed …
Harps tuned … Hearts filled up with love.

—Sign seen in a hospital

The first hope in our inventory—
the hope that includes and at the same time
transcends all others—must be the hope
that love is going to have the last word.

—Arnold Toynbee

The source of love is deep in us, and we can
call upon it to help others. One word, one action,
one loving thought can reduce another person's
suffering and bring that person joy.

—Thich Nhat Hanh

BECAUSE

When I was about to start my second bone marrow transplant, I received a big basket. It was from my beloved nurse, Mara. Inside the basket were 21 gift-wrapped packages of all shapes and sizes. She had sent instructions to open one each day. Regardless of what else the day had in store for me, my basket from Mara held the promise of a gift of love just for me—a crossword puzzle, hand lotion, a flavored lip gloss. Each one touched my heart and gave me strength for the fight. Thank you, Mara, for loving me and caring about me.

—Vickie Girard, Cancer Survivor

YOUCARE

Love cures people—both the ones who
give it and the ones who receive it.

—Dr. Karl Menninger

If I told patients to raise their blood levels of
immune globulins or killer T-cells, no one would
know how. But if I can teach them to love
themselves and others fully, the same change
happens automatically. The truth is: Love heals.

—Bernie Siegel, MD

The more unloving a patient acts,
the more he needs to be loved.

—Sally Karioth, RN

BECAUSE

If you quit loving the moment
it becomes difficult, you never
discover compassion.

— David Augsburger

The most loving thing you
do today will most likely be the
hardest thing you do.

— Keynote

Don't forget to love yourself.

— Soren Kierkegaard

YOUCARE

A year ago I thought I would never walk again. Today I walked the beach with my four year old on my shoulders. There were tears in my eyes, but we were both laughing out loud. How can I ever thank you?

HEALING

In a world of high tech,
we still need high touch.

—Steve Siemens

When we hear the word "hospital,"
technology and scientific invention spring to
mind...(but) there are other, equally important life
supports in our healthcare system: the 2.2 million
nurses who make up the profession. These women
and men weave a tapestry of care, knowledge,
and trust that is critical to patients' survival.

—Suzanne Gordon,
"What Nurses Stand For"

The greatest mistake in the treatment of diseases is that there are physicians for the body and physicians for the soul, although the two cannot be separated.

—Plato

I am here. Let's heal together.

—A Nurse

Too often we underestimate the power of a touch, a smile, a kind word, a listening ear, or the smallest act of caring.

—Leo Buscaglia

BECAUSE

Constant attention by a good nurse
may be just as important as a major
operation by a surgeon.

— Dag Hammarskjold

Healing the spirit is as
important as healing the body.

— Sally Karioth, RN

Nurses have the unique opportunity
to direct the healing experience. They are
the bridges between humanity and medical
machines. They can say it all by sitting
quietly at a bedside and saying nothing.

— Deb Tarara, RN

YOUCARE

Take good care of yourself...
so you can take good care of others.

—Hospice Volunteer

We have to look after our own
health—those of us who have so
long looked after the health of others.

—Maya Angelou

Be kind, compassionate and gentle...
with yourself. You are needed.

—Dick Anderson

BECAUSE

In helping others, we shall help ourselves,
for whatever good we give out completes
the circle and comes back to us.

— Flora Edwards

What I do you cannot do; but what you do,
I cannot do. The needs are great, and none of us,
including me, ever do great things. But we can
do small things, with great love, and together
we can do something wonderful.

— Mother Teresa

YOUCARE

I don't like hospitals and
I don't do well with pain.
How you put up with me I
will never know. Please
extend my sincere thanks to
all the nurses on Floor 9.
You know who they are —
the ones with the wings.

PATIENCE

Nurses have lots of patients.

—Anonymous

If you can keep your head when all
about you are losing theirs and blaming it
on you...chances are, you're a nurse.

—Lifelines

"Talk about the patience of Job,"
said a hospital nurse,
"Job was never on night duty!"

—Stephen Paget

RN means real nice.

—Greeting Card

True patience is not just something
you do, it's something you don't do. I can
walk again because my doctors and nurses
didn't give up on me, didn't snap back
at me, didn't lose faith in me.

—Ryan Holt

Never to tire, never to grow cold; to be
patient, sympathetic, tender; to look
for the opening heart; to hope always,
to love always—this is our duty.

—H.F. Amiel

BECAUSE

Be patient with everyone,
but above all with yourself.

— St. Francis de Sales

Feel warm and loving toward yourself,
for you are a unique and precious person,
ever doing the best your awareness permits,
ever growing in wisdom and love.

— Keynote

By having the courage to be yourself,
you put something wonderful in the
world that was not there before.

— Edwin Elliot

YOUCARE

Bright star, if only I were
as steadfast as you.

—Elizabeth David

Most of this world's useful work is done
by people who are pressed for time, or are
tired, or don't feel well. One may still go a
long way after one is tired.

—Unknown

When you put yourself wholeheartedly
into something, energy grows.
It seems inexhaustible.

—Helen de Rosis

BECAUSE

The weariest night, the longest day,
sooner or later must come to an end.

— Baroness Orczy

Being a nurse you see life in a
different light. The night seems so
dark and the morning so bright.

— Dawn Butler

Have courage for the great sorrows of life,
and patience for the small ones; and when you
have finally accomplished your daily task,
go to sleep in peace. God is awake.

— Victor Hugo

YOUCARE

For two weeks I watched the nurses come and go. One night I'm laying there in my hospital gown thinking, "You know what? These people have it figured out. I make lots of money, but they make a better world."

WISDOM

Time has a wonderful way of
showing us what really matters.

—Margaret Peters

The things that matter most
in this world, they can never
be held in our hand.

—Gloria Gaither

It is not what we get, but who
we become, what we contribute...
that gives meaning to our lives.

—Anthony Robbins

All of us must learn this
lesson somewhere—that it costs
something to be what we are.

—Shirley Abbott

Life owes us little; we owe it everything.
The only true happiness comes from
squandering ourselves for a purpose.

—John Marm Brown

I've learned that what we have done for
ourselves alone dies with us. What we
have done for others and the world
remains and is immortal.

—Unknown

BECAUSE

What wisdom can you find that
is greater than kindness?

—Jean Jacques Rousseau

Those who make compassion an essential
part of their lives find the joy of life. Kindness
deepens the spirit and produces rewards that
cannot be completely explained in words.

—Robert J. Furey

It is one of the most beautiful
compensations of this life that you
cannot sincerely try to help another
without helping yourself.

—Ralph Waldo Emerson

YOUCARE

Not he who has much is rich,
but he who gives much.

—Erich Fromm

You are richer today if you
have laughed, given, comforted,
healed or forgiven.

—Jack Bongioni, MD

Don't confuse fame with success.
Madonna is one; Helen Keller is the other.

—Erma Bombeck

BECAUSE

I will love the light for it shows me
the way, yet I will endure the darkness
for it shows me the stars.

—Og Mandino

I'm a nurse. Both my parents eventually
died of cancer, but we learned many things
together along the way. In our last days together,
I learned to speak a new language with great
clarity. It's a language that cancer doesn't
understand, can't comprehend—a language
of love, hope, faith, dignity and courage.

—Marcia Peterson

YOUCARE

We know you were helping to deliver other babies that night, but you made us feel like ours was the only one. Honestly, I don't know how you hold up — you were with us every step of the way.

STRENGTH

Nothing makes us feel so
strong as a call for help.

—George MacDonald

Strength is granted to us
all when we are needed to
serve great causes.

—Winston Churchill

We are never asked to do more
than we are able without being given
the strength and ability to do it.

—Eileen Caddy

She is strong who laughs
at herself and cries for others.

—Don Ward

Nothing is so strong as gentleness;
nothing so gentle as real strength.

—St. Frances de Sales

I was always looking outside myself
for strength and confidence, but it comes
from within. It is there all the time.

—Anna Freud

BECAUSE

The human spirit is stronger
than anything that can happen to it.
—George C. Scott

If children with terminal cancer
can find love, joy, beauty and strength in
their day—and they do—we can too.
—Dan Zadra

Have a heart that never hardens,
a love that never tires, and a
touch that never hurts.
—Charles Dickens

YOUCARE

Never despair, but if you do,
work on in despair.
—Edmund Burke

Sometimes we cry 'cause
we can't save them all,
God sometimes won't let
us interfere when He calls.
—Dawn Butler

Tears may be dried up,
but the heart—never.
—Marguerite De Valois

BECAUSE

Just pray for a tough
hide and a tender heart.

—Ruth Graham

Please give me the strength to face the day ahead.
Please give me courage, as I approach each
hurting bed…Please give me assurance, as the
day slips into night, that I have done the best
I can, that I have done what's right.

—A Nurse's Prayer

Have faith. God's care will carry you…
so you can carry others.

—Dr. Robert Schuller

YOUCARE

WHEN I FELT I NEEDED A
MIRACLE, THE HOSPITAL
CHAPLAIN SAID, "LOOK, WE
SEE MIRACLES ALL THE
TIME AROUND HERE.
WHERE THERE IS GREAT
LOVE, THERE ARE ALWAYS
MIRACLES."

MIRACLES

Unselfish acts are the real
miracles out of which all the
reported miracles grow.

—Ralph Waldo Emerson

I've seen and met angels
wearing the disguise of ordinary
people living ordinary lives.

—Tracy Chapman

An elderly woman describing the nursing
staff at Seattle's Swedish Hospital:
"If you ask, an angel appears."

—Bernadette Flynn

Kind words can be short
and easy to speak, but their
echoes are truly endless.

—Mother Teresa

When we do the best we can, we
never know what miracle is wrought
in our life, or in the life of another.

—Helen Keller

Every action of our lives
touches on some chord that
will vibrate in Eternity.

—Edwin Hubbel Chapin

BECAUSE

The effect of one good-hearted
person is incalculable.

—Oscar Arias

How long does it take for you
to stop, smile and lift someone's
spirits? Just a tiny little minute.
But Eternity is in it.

—Mary Augustine

Kindness is a language
that the deaf can hear
and the blind can see.

—Mark Twain

YOUCARE

Know that you yourself
are a miracle.

—Norman Vincent Peale

The trained nurse has given
nursing the divine touch.

—Charles H. Mayo

I see their souls, and I hold them
in my hands, and because I love
them they weigh nothing.

—Pearl Bailey

BECAUSE

It is up to you to illuminate the world.

—Philippe Venier

We won't always know whose
lives we touched and made better for
our having cared. What's important is
that you do care and you act.

—Charlotte Lunsford

The miracle is not that
we do this work, but that
we are happy to do it.

—Mother Teresa

YOUCARE

You guys remind me of the old M.A.S.H television show. You are quirky and wonderful and caring — a bunch of characters who laugh and cry and save lives. Where would we be without you?

HERO

We relish news of our
heroes, forgetting that we are
extraordinary to someone too.

—Helen Hayes

A hero is someone who has
given his life to something
bigger than himself.

—Joseph Campbell

No person was ever honored
for what he received. Honor has
been the reward for what he gave.

—Calvin Coolidge

Everywhere in life the true
question is not what we have
gained, but what we do.

—Thomas Carlyle

Just 200 years ago the average
American died by age 35. Today, we give
new hearts, lungs and eyes to our loved ones.
Together we've conquered smallpox, polio and
cholera—and we will soon conquer cancer.

—Don Ward

BECAUSE

We need to teach our children that
not all heroes are honored in a big parade.
There are everyday people all across the country—
doctors, nurses and their patients—who are
quietly battling serious illness, and whose courage
would easily eclipse the caped crusaders'.

—Stronger Than Cancer

Do your little bit of good where
you are; it's those little bits of good
put together that overwhelm the world.

—Archbishop Desmond Tutu

YOUCARE

The world will be saved by
one or two people at a time.

—Andre Gide

You must behave as if your
everyday act, even the smallest,
impacted a thousand people for a
hundred generations. Because it does.

—Herr Mueller

We ourselves feel that what we
are doing is just a drop in an ocean.
But the ocean would be less
because of that missing drop.

—Mother Teresa

BECAUSE

Sorry if we woke you in the middle of the night,
But someone in your neighborhood is fighting for his life.
Sorry if we block the road and make you turn around,
But there's been a bad wreck with
dying children on the ground.
When you see us coming you'll understand,
Let us have the right-of-way, someone
needs a helping hand.
We don't do it for the money—you know we don't get paid.
We don't do it for the glory but for
the life that might be saved.
Somewhere deep within us our souls are crying out
"We're here to help our neighbors in
their hour of pain and doubt."
God gave us something special to help us see you through,
We do it 'cause we love you, and we care about you too.

—Unknown

YOU CARE

Forget yourself for others,
and others will never forget you.

— Unknown

Wherever you go, nurses are the unsung
heroes of the cancer brigade. They are the ones
who provide "just what the doctor orders," and so
much more. They can fix a broken stitch, or mend
a broken heart. I know, because I had a nurse
mend my heart several times during my
husband, Walter's, tragic illness.

— Connie Payton

BECAUSE

How far your little candle
throws its beams!

— William Shakespeare

You really can change the
world if you care enough.

— Marian Wright Edelman

It's a great satisfaction
knowing that for a brief point in
time you made a difference.

— Irene Natividad

YOUCARE

To know even one life
has breathed easier
because you have lived;
that is to have succeeded.

—Ralph Waldo Emerson